IT'S
TOUGH BEING A
GROWN UP!

IT'S TOUGH BEING A GROWN UP!

Malika Bhandarkar

atmosphere press

Thank you for all your love
And all the encouragement too
Thank you for standing by me
I'm so lucky I can count on you

To my champions and my heart
Usha and Ashok Bhandarkar
Jeevan and Aadi Venkataswamy

Foreword

Welcome, welcome, welcome in!
I've been waiting to sit by you

Come twinkle and gasp and escape with me
We'll laugh and weave fables anew

Reimagining our world by your side
O what new thinks we will debut!

Contents

Rewriting the Rules

Report Card 5
Plan Aerobics 6
Fortunes Told 8
Conditions 10

Assumptions

Netflix, You Got Me Wrong 13
Pounce-ciations 14
Brand Identity for Baby 16
I'm Not A Pigeon 20
Amitabh 22
Colonizers Guide to Self-Awareness 24

Middle Age

Tummy Worship 29
The Importance of Name Tags 30
Hullaballoo 32
Scented 34
A Dream or a Promise? 35
BLT Ban 36
A Squeak 38
Memories 39

Affairs of the Heart

I Love What You Love 43
First Date, with My Very Own Harry Styles 44
Plates & Bowls 46
The Answer Is Yes 48
An Affair 51
Blue 52
Listening in Quatrain 53
Wrapped 54

Mind Your Manners

Concerto at Lunch   57
A Trail   58
Herbivore Rumble   60
Velcro Friends   61
Couldn't Be Me   62

Kid Aches

Lepidoptera Census   67
Cucumber Sandwiches   68
There Is Nothing Quite Like a Dog   70
Protected   72
Social Media Safari   75
Good Company   76
Sleuthing   78
Number One Auntie   80
Magic Carpet   82

Vexations

What Will You Be?   87
Circles   88
Kite   90
Skyline   91
Outgrown   92
Duelling in Verse   94

Acknowledgements

About the Author

Rewriting
the Rules

Report Card

Will it say I'm helpful?
Will it say I'm kind?
Will it tell of how I helped a friend
Out of her lunchbox bind?

Will it remember the scars I earned
When I tripped and fell?
Will it show how good my balance is?
How at hide and seek I excel?

Will they give me marks for questions?
Or only the answers I knew?
I learned more from every question I asked
From my answers, very few

Do I get an A+ for being me?
Or embracing the breeze?
Does it only count if put in words?
And what does an A+ guarantee?

Plan Aerobics

I've always had a plan
Since I was ten and two
A plan and decision tree
That would see me through

A plan for work and play
A plan and a list
To do the things I loved:
Nothing would be missed

I had a decision tree
That spanned two dozen years
Laden with options and ideas
Shining with prompts and steers

I'd live a life of purpose
And always have time to dance
Be patient with the grunt work
Do new things, every chance

I was having too much fun
Living life and learning its rules
And ran out of a plan
Now left wondering what to do

Not everything went to plan
It's true it was 50-50
Though I never lost my way
It's time to do a gear-shifty

All the things I love most
Weren't part of the plan
Not the friends or destinations
Not my radiant man

So if fifty of the plan
Got me to the fifty I love
Which fifty should I keep
And which fifty should I shove?

Time for a reset
Time to breathe
Or time to let go
Or live at double speed?

Fortunes Told

I am a fortune teller
Would you like your fortune told?
I have good news, and plenty of truths:
Life ahead will be bright and bold

Today is going to be wonderful
Good in every way
It's good because you decided
That nothing will get in your way

I used to wear a turban
But it made my head itch
Hazy are crystals, stars and palms
So to "will power" did I switch

Why worry about the stars?
They are dancing to their own tune
Follow your bliss and you will find
They will follow you and swoon

You know I'm right, as right can be
There is no question here
For self-fulfilling prophecies
Show mind over matter, my dear

Believe in me my friend
For I believe in you
There is nothing that is impossible
There's nothing you cannot do

Conditions

I can't eat gluten or rice
So quinoa it must be
I forget why: is it trendy?
Or do I have an allergy?

I must sleep by nine
To have a good day
Though when I dance till two
My soul with joy sways

I need to walk forty minutes
Or my machinery is stuck
But if I walk sixty
My energy is out of luck

My conditions have conditions
And I can't remember them all
So all my conditions have exceptions
And gosh I'm having a ball!

Assumptions

Netflix, You Got Me Wrong

Your algorithm has got me wrong
I didn't realise before I fell
Down a rabbit hole of "movies I'd like"
Into an echo chamber hell

Netflix you lost me at
"Movies like this"
If I've seen it before
I'd like to give it a miss

Has it been remade in German?
I've got to see it, I say with a twinge
You've tricked me again Netflix
Foiled by my own weakness to binge

Comedy, military history and sci-fi
All genres interest me
Does life have a genre?
That I'm yet to see

Stop telling me what I like
I want to go exploring
I want to learn something new each day
Let my curiosity stay, I'm imploring

Pounce-ciations

Folks do tend to pounce
If per chance you mispronounce
With corrections immediately announced

I didn't mind
When you said my name wrong
Mistaking it for an African pop song

Does it really matter
How you say a word?
Pronunciations are quite absurd

Shift a timezone
Or a latitude
Suddenly 'E's in hats are all about attitude

Is my 'A' too flat?
Or didn't I roll my 'R'?
Linguistic acrobatics are bizarre

The snooty use it
As a "class" detector
Forgetting it's ideas that are nectar

Did you like the story?
Did you think it good?
All anyone wants is to be understood

Brand Identity for Baby*

Your name is a wonder
Do you love it too?
It shows the love and care taken
In hand picking it – just for you

Every name spells love
No matter the letters in it
No matter how you sound it out
It echoes with love within it

You may be entrusted with a legacy
A name generations old
Or something more precious than
Bitcoins, jade or gold

Perhaps you are a rhyme
With a sibling, twin or kin
Or a virtue or action hero
That makes the world grin

***Note:** What's in a name? Often instant judgement unbeknownst to the newly introduced – Is she truly Grace-ful? How divine is he really? – when instead it signifies a nomenclature of hope, by loving parents with rose tinted glasses.*

Your name may be divine
In hopes of bringing heaven to earth
Or a royal warrior or statesman
Championing justice and worth

Perhaps you are a lyric
Or a flower with a scent so sweet
Or a poet-philosopher-inspirer
Making the world complete

It wasn't a joke or misquote
When your name was selected
It was crowd sourced, argued, spell-checked and bully-proofed
Elected after hundreds rejected

When a check on Google Translate
Results in something rude
The names have to be nixed
(Glad we didn't get tattooed!)

Your name is very special
It can be very unique
Your parents had never seen anything like you
They're sure the world has now peaked

There are names that
Made me laugh, with quips pointed
But now I remember the hopeful *namers*
you are their ambassador of dreams, anointed

Your name
It's been used to coax a smile
And an extra helping at dinner
It's been said jubilantly
Whenever you arrive
For family, you are a winner

Your name has been echoed lovingly
Around the world in prayer:
May love light your way
May your wishes come true
May you be noble and kind
In all that you do
May your heart always be peaceful
FOMO-, YOLO-, label-free
May serendipity be your companion
May there be joy in everything you see

After all that effort
Invariably additions are made
By kith, kin and kooks
Begins a nick name parade

Sometimes a diminutive
Cooed with love expanding
Sometimes a playground pun
Spent a lifetime rebranding

And when you've lived, and lived well
I hope you'll be able to say
"I've given my name new meaning
By deed, word and fair play
There's never been a Rembrandt like me
Nor has there been a Sue
I've made my name famous"
                I wonder what new planet,
                bear species
                critter or city, they will name after you?

I'm Not A Pigeon

What? When? Why?
Questions without a pause
All asked before a reply
Perhaps you prefer applause?

At first, I was excited
O how we'd swap stories and grow
Now I find you're not curious an iota
Building walls around the little you know

Your questions are a mirror
To your mind
      Your heart
           Your fear
The verdict decided before the answer
You're stuck in an echo chamber dear

You're wondering which pigeon hole I fit
You're looking for all the clues
You're wondering if I'm worth talking to
Now I'm wondering about you

Your repetitiveness makes me curious
Do you only know one tune?
Did you choose it for fear or comfort?
Like an ostrich head in a sand dune?

I'm starting to see a trend
And it's not a promising one
You're turning me into you:
Passing judgement on everyone

Amitabh*

In the mountains I heard a song
A song I'd heard before
In a language I didn't understand
a-n-y-m-o-r-e

But my heart it filled with joy
And my feet they tapped in tune
This was a song I knew
For my soul a happy boon

There came a big warm laugh
Drumming the wheel to the beat
"Do you know Amitabh?"
Said the man from the front seat

"I don't understand his words
I know not what he sings in song
But they speak to me they do
And I always hum along"

In Sierra Leone I sat
I couldn't believe my ears
Bollywood had given me an ice breaker
Though I hadn't seen a movie in years

*Note: Amitabh refers to Amitabh Bachchan – one of India's top Bollywood actors, who has surprisingly held that spot and enthralled his fan base for over 40 years. Much like Tom Cruise of Hollywood today.

Colonizers Guide to Self-Awareness

What gave you the impression
Perhaps it's a legacy of deception
That we need to be saved?

Let me correct that assumption
A colonial malfunction
There isn't anything we can't brave

You talk of disadvantage
And worry we can't compete
But it's you who made the rules

We outstripped your GDP
Outpacing every industry
Don't take us for a fool

You redrew our borders
Pitted us against each other
Undermining us at every stage

Your boundless greed for power
Etched centuries of repercussions
But we won't give up on a golden age

Your racist, sexist attitudes
Can't be obscured by platitudes
You're resting on the laurels of yore

If you speak to us as equals
This relationship will have a sequel
Even though you're a special kind of bore

You've imported our
CEOs, cricketers, yoga, and curry
It took centuries: now you're learning about us in a hurry

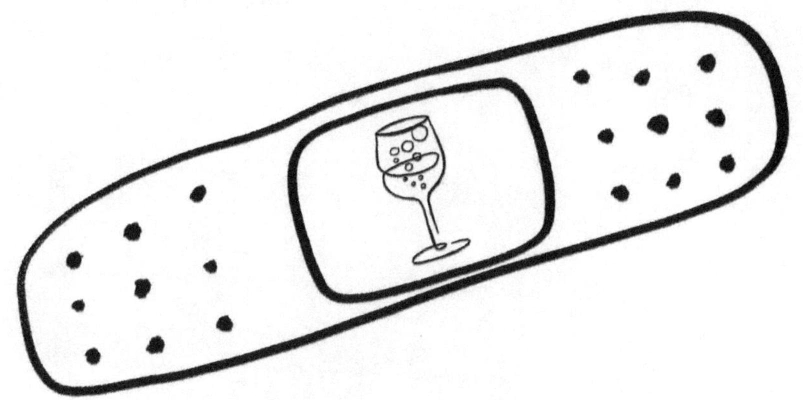

Middle Age

Tummy Worship

It is too late
I see the rise of the *pait**
Was there gluten at tea?
Did I eat dairy? Or sugar or cream?
Perhaps I swallowed a bee?

You see I was distracted with your stories
And all the laughter we shared
Six sandwiches you say?
With a chocolate milkshake?
Washed down without a care

**Translation note: Pait is tummy in Hindi.*

The Importance of Name Tags

Hello there! How are you?
It's so good to see you after all these years!
I nod and say "How true, how true
Tell me about you, I'd love to hear"

My brain is scanning furiously
By year, by date, by group
Were we friends in school?
Or in a cooking class making soup?

Did I train her in Uganda?
Or do a panel in New York?
Did we meet online during Covid?
Or at a safari of storks?

Perhaps she is my mother's friend?
Or my father's classmate?
Perhaps she is the sister
Of the boy I fleetingly date?

Is she the new wife
Of an old college friend?
Did we chat at a wedding
About life, love, and the end?

Has she mistaken me
For someone else? Another?
That would be a relief
How can this truth I uncover?

We're talking of headlines
Not a hint dropped, let's be frank
Of a common friend or colleague
Your name is still: blank

Would it be very impolite
To look up LinkedIn or Facebook?
But what is her name?
How do you look up a look?

Hullaballoo

I am an only child
And I have only one name
You've known it since we met
No, it's not Garry or Gail

It's not Jeremy or Nick
One thinks you don't care
Not John or Jack or Tom
How do you put me in your prayers?

I feel rather incomplete
When you call me Pete
No, it's not Pietro or Pedro
Why is this name on repeat?

Not Paul or Adam
That trended for a while
Not Ed, Rob, or Mani
(I'm trying to hide my smile)

Are you having me on?
Did you learn this from my Mum?
Today she called me every name
But mine, under the sun

No, it's not Katie or Liz
You're renaming me again
By the last person who called
No, no, it's not Ben

I should be very cross
Yes, very, very mad
But your innocent proclamations
Are like a bad memory ad

How is it, pray tell
That my name escapes you?
I wear it on a necklace
I'll make it font size 82

You think as an only child
And his only wife too
I'd get VIP treatment
Instead of a name hullabaloo

Scented

A beautiful scent fills the air
Where does it come from, O where?
I feel like I'm living in the Arabian Nights
Jasmine wafts in rooms so light

This fragrant potpourri
Simply can't be me
Today I haven't spritzed
This giddy scent has me miffed

Is it patchouli I'm sniffing?
Or oranges and roses blooming?
Is it yours?
My goodness, now I smell it outdoors

Not an orchard or moon garden in sight
How am I blessed with this Arabian night?
I've followed this perfume for days
Through cars, bars, and market maze

I whip around
The source is found
I'm embarrassed to admit
That my new hair conditioner is the culprit

A Dream or a Promise?

A promise I had made
The one I'd said I'd keep
A secret you had whispered
While I was half asleep

I thought it was a dream
What an intriguing plot
You were lounging on the beach
The sun was bubbling hot

A spy did you say?
A sniper as well?
A hiccup changed a boundary
Warring countries did it spell

"Promise," you begged
"Not a soul will you tell
About my reckless past,
My blunder, my hell"

I nodded yes
And I meant it, too
It slips out now and then...
Like today, out of the blue

BLT Ban

No BLT
No BLT
Said the doctor very pointedly

No BLT
No BLT
That sounds as easy can be

Not a sandwich?
Then what could it be?
Doctor, can you spell it out for me?

No bending, no lifting
No twisting
Three rules on which I'm insisting

Thought it would be a cinch
And then... on the floor it fell
The only pen: Adieu, farewell

Also my favourite flavour
Of chips are stored
Behind the cabinet's lowest door

So, I wiggled my toes
Turning them into grips
Tackled the pen and packet of chips

I'm holding onto my sanity
Months of no BLT
Have made a monkey out of me

A Squeak

A squeak, a squawk, a trill
A sound too divine or shrill
Time and perspective decide
If you greet or hide

At the window scanning the sea
Serene with fish and stork
A squawk is given a D
While prepping for exams on quarks

Same room, same time, same glance
Same squawker per chance
Two decades later, ears rejoice
Parrots and kites are paradise

Deadlines, calls and meetings
Your ears hear a cooing, so fleeting
Or was it a gurgle and whine
For a welcome break you pine

Tuning out is an art to be mastered
To weather any noisy disaster
Seek in it joy with an open mind
Now you're the master's master divine

Memories

The patter of feet in quick succession
Small, light, numerous
The twitter of voices in hesitation
Giggling, sweet, melodious.

The happiness of seventh heaven
Calm, complete, satisfying
The curiosity of a nosy raven
Mischievous, sharp, probing

The scent of chocolate cake
Warm, delicious and lush
Untangling a mass of curls
Gently with a soft brush

All this will disappear
A new life will appear
All the past but a memory
For the child it will be

Affairs
of the Heart

I Love What You Love

When you tell me of your grandma
And how she gave you hugs
When you tell me beautiful stories
Always so filled with love
My heart it swells with joy
It grows and grows and grows
My love it gets bigger
To love everyone you know

When you tell me stories of cats
O how I love them too
I've only ever known dogs
Now I know cats through you
You see their warmth and beauty
And cherish their naughty winks
So my heart grows again
Boom zwink zwink zwink

You told me of your friend:
Kind and sweet and brave
I didn't like him much –
What a silly knave
But your love for him is steadfast
And you champion him no matter what
Now I love him too
His weakness quite forgot

Every day I find
I love more and more and more
So keep telling me stories
Can't wait to see what's in store!

First Date, with My Very Own Harry Styles

I never had a list
Except tall and sweet
I never expected this
Until you, did I meet

I don't date beards
(Literal and figuratively)
Nor fellas who are
Younger than me

I never cancel plans
Especially for a guy
But I'm making exceptions
And I don't know why

We're chatting over tea
(You remember I don't drink)
We're making plans already
And I like your ink

It's been four hours
Now it's been eight
It's a chat-walk-dance-a-thon
And only our first date

We talk of candies and loss
And everything in-between
There are walking silences too
We know exactly what they mean

You like strong women
I like smart men, with open minds
Your family is matriarchal
What a gem! What a find!

You turned into my list
Soft curls and easy laughs
I'm glad you popped the question
Though it took three years and a half

Plates & Bowls

I like to eat in bowls
He likes to eat on plates
Separately we are always on time
Together often late

Both of us should wear glasses
Neither of us do
Sunny or muted we can't decide
Both of us like blue

Action, horror, biographies
He can't get enough
We both love philosophy
Mine rhymes, his is tough

He loves strings and melodies
Lyrics are a must in my songs
He likes dramas, we adore parodies
How do we get along?

He loves to run and run
Dancing is my bliss
We both love ice cream
And are sad to give it a miss

He loves games of all stripes
Chooses cricket over golf swings
I'll watch games and cheer loudly
He says only ticket holders should sing

He never turns his phone off
Mine is always on mute
He never forgets his keys
I'm often saying "Oh, shoot!"

His hair is beautiful and curly
Mine fluffy and straight
He takes his time to get ready
And I'm happy to wait

He loves tigers who roar
I love nature in all her bloom
We'd rather walk, not hike
Pollen is our doom

Words are my joy
Action is his truth
He rejoices in recipes
I like stories with a sleuth

What a perfect match
So much to discuss and learn
Where next to dine and how to dress?
It depends on whose turn

The Answer Is Yes

Yes, I will come play with you
Yes, let's go exploring
Yes, let's lie on the grass
Yes, let's dance when it's pouring

Yes, I want to hear your stories
Yes, your sorrows too
Yes, we'll laugh them away
As only buddies know how to do

Yes, let's travel the world
Yes, I'll go to Timbuktu
Yes, I'll calypso in Jamaica
As long as it's with you

Yes, let's start with ice cream
Yes, let's eat biryani next
Yes, let's get Pepto-Bismol
Yes, I'll answer all your texts

Yes, I'll listen to a string quartet
Yes, I'll jig to Taylor Swift
Yes, I'll do the World Science Fest
With you, I love getting miffed

Yes, I'll put the flowers out
Yes, I'll clean up for the guests
Yes, I've laid out the bar
Yes, I'll take care of the rest

Yes, we'll write our own rules
Yes, we'll turn off our phones
Yes, we'll play hooky
Yes, we'll skip stones

Yes, I'll watch cricket
Yes, I'll cheer at football too
Yes, I'll be surprised by tennis
Yes, I'll google their rules

Yes, I'll come to your doctor
Yes, I'll hold your hand
Yes, we'll take it step by step
Yes, I'll join you for a scan

Yes, let's think of yesterday
Yes, let's plan for tomorrow
Yes, let's dream our day away
Yes, let's a llama borrow

Every time you ask
The answer will always be yes
It's you I love the most
Didn't you already guess?

Marry, you say?
This may come as a blow
We're already having so much fun
The answer is no

An Affair

There is a rumour going round
I'm having an affair
With a man with no facial hair

It took me by surprise
It got me wondering aloud
Is the man I'm cavorting with in this crowd?

The penny dropped when
You were laughing by my side
And the gossip realised you'd shaved and dyed

Blue

Today I don't want to be funny
Today I don't want to be smart
Today I want to be just me
Right from the start

Today I am little sad
The sunshine still has me blue
Today I'm thinking of all the "could've beens"
That could've been with you

Today, I am thinking of tomorrows
And all the tomorrows to come
And it makes me sad that you won't be around
To join in any one

The tomorrows make my heart heavy
They make every bit of me ache
I don't like the tomorrow
Where you're not part of the stake

Give me a moment to be woeful
And a moment to grieve
Before I close the door to tomorrow
And join you for a walk by the sea

Listening in Quatrain

Foolishness

If you don't agree with me
Then I'm not listening to you
If you agree, then
There's no listening to do

Quietude, or Dear, Why the Silent Treatment?

If there is no one to talk to
Will I still have something to say?
If there is no one to listen
Will my thoughts just melt away?

Wrapped

She is wrapped around my finger
My mittens are on his heart
It doesn't matter if we're together
Or far far apart

One look is all it takes
A soft whisper is all I need
Just the crook of my finger
And my wish is their deed

They think they're training me
My parents, so naïve
With sleep schedules
Planned activities and feeds

I've quietly coached them
(With a coo, it's guaranteed)
Hopping to my whims
At double triple speed

Mind
Your Manners

Concerto at Lunch

He must think he is charming
Yes, quite disarming
Look how he projects with a grin

He must think it beguiling
Because I am still smiling
from shock...

          ... at his orchestra burping din

A Trail

Do you like Sherlock Holmes?
Is that why you're leaving clues?
Your prints are everywhere
From your head to your shoes

There are fingerprints on the couch
From when you ate chips
Head prints on the cushion
When your hair with oil drips

Footprints on the silk carpet
Of your gliding toes
A trail of crumbs from the kitchen
To wherever you go

These marks are turning
Into house tattoos
At least make it difficult
For Holmes to catch you

Maybe it's a Hansel-Gretel Complex
Thinking you'd be forgotten or lost
Please shake off this perception
Your trail in the apartment is embossed

That stain?
Isn't that you too?
Me? Oh my, on the bus
I must've sat on paint and glue

Herbivore Rumble

Just because I am quiet
And on a plant diet
Doesn't mean I can't take you on

I am smart, I am able
Don't think me a vegetable
Allow me to prove how strong

I have a poet's heart
And am lioness in part
Watch out for my pouncing song

Now I've got you beat
And in quick retreat
You won't be treating herbivores wrong

Velcro Friends*

I have a book
But I want to read yours

I have a plan
But I'll join your detour

I have a phone
But I'd rather see your screen

The grass is greener on the other side?
I don't know what you mean

Note: *An unshakable friend, colleague, amour or acquaintance can stick like Velcro to you and your plans. Sometimes an act of love, often of admiration but decidedly an unwelcome overture.*

Couldn't Be Me

Thank you for coming
To this press conference
I need to clear the air
I'm pro business, pro trees
Pro labour, pro bees
So let me say this with care

It couldn't be me!
I'm green through and through
All I wear is sustainably sourced
My campaign is all about equality
Not fluff, waste or frivolity
Fairness and equity are enforced

I've had a press secretary
She wasn't appointed by me
Since I was a day old
She ran all my media feeds
Took care of all my needs
She's my mother
And can't be controlled

It is very apparent
My life has been transparent
Uploaded for all to see
Didn't know I had rights
Was still figuring out tights
She didn't turn on settings privacy

No matter what I pledge
There is already a wedge
Thanks to my silver spoon and wasteful clan
For my romper of cashmere
And hired planes and reindeer
I promise it's all now a ban

Though I'm smiling and composed
I have definitely been exposed
I couldn't curate my content
Every tantrum has been seen
With commentary routine
For my parents – time well spent

Your arguments have a base
I did move with malaise
When I was a teen, and sulk
I have grown, I have changed
My persona re-arranged
To family guy sans hulk

I didn't know then
What I know now
I have a career picked
I'd like to be your nominee
For the country presidency
Vote for me quick

Kid Aches

Lepidoptera Census

I've been watching butterflies
Big bright yellow ones
Flitting from flower to flower
Shining in the sun

I'm counting all the butterflies
And I'll give you the reason
It's because I've been protecting
Caterpillars all season

Cucumber Sandwiches

Cucumber sandwiches are great
When you are seventy-eight
They sit elegantly in your fingers at tea

But when you're just seven
O gosh! O heaven!
They are terrible 'break time' currency

No one would swap
Not even one sticky lollipop
For ten sandwiches – that's a guarantee

I complained to my Mum
Saying this just wasn't done
This lunchbox would be the end of me

She only half heard
Because on the third
I had chopped carrots and celery

Have you every tried to dip
A celery stick
In garlic yogurt from a boxed lunch?

It clears out the bench
With the crunch and stench
While you sit there alone and munch

Then suddenly one day
Hip Hip Hooray!
I got chocs and chips and jam

Now I'm as hungry as can be
Though my box is empty
They gobbled up my lunch and ran

There Is Nothing Quite Like a Dog

I asked and asked and asked
And prayed and prayed and prayed
Every day offering sweets and trades

I thought I had won
I thought it had worked
Behind my Dad, a big box lurked

I opened it gleefully
How lucky am I!
I'll soon have my very own puppy ally

It was fluffy indeed
But it didn't twitch
A stuffed cat emerged. Another hitch!

I wandered about for weeks
A red ribbon deftly tied
To a sliding fluffy cat by my side

"A walking talking fellow"
Said my father indulgently
"Hooray!" I cried triumphantly

A sausage dog emerged
Sweet, yappy and fun
His batteries went down with the sun

I haven't given up
Not one bit. Not yet
I bring home everyone else's pets

Are they beginning to soften?
Wait! The plan needs to back up
They want to REPLACE ME with a pup!

Protected

Surrounded by turrets and minarets
Sitting high up in her tower
Watching the world at play
Was a princess O so dour

She wasn't allowed anywhere
For fear she'd trip and fall
So the poor princess, with all her riches
Went nowhere at all

She would sigh a big sigh
When to the theatre she'd go
Cosseted in the royal box
With her smile so faux

She was made to sit alone
So bugs didn't have a chance
To spare her sprained ankles
She wasn't allowed to dance

All her meals were bland
For fear of tummy trouble
The princess was dismayed
With her imperial bubble

Books were her only adventure
Along with pen pal letters
Every read made her braver
Her plan for escape better

Then one day, as she sat
Dreaming of magic carpets and rings
Her imagination burnt so bright
She sprouted iridescent wings

She clapped her hands with glee
And wrote her parents a note
"I love you, but I've flown the coop
Adios." End quote

In mid-air she pirouetted
And flew off like a gale
Leaving behind her cage of treasures
And her palatial jail

Now we see her on TV
She's a doctor, chef, imagineer
CEO of Great Escapes
And a deep space pioneer

T-shirts are printed with her quotes:
"I can do impossible things
I will always bounce back.
Imagination gives you wings!"

Social Media Safari

I met a quokka on YouTube
And how he made me laugh
He loved selfies – you just had to ask

And on TikTok was a tree kangaroo
Relishing her red grapes
Smilingly planning her great escape

A documentary on kakapos
Was the best of all
Heaviest parrots in the world, having a ball

I've fallen in love with the quetzal
And its three-foot tail
How long will it take to Costa Rica if I sail?

I'd love to meet all these new friends
From across the earth
Can't I pay my fare in rhymes and mirth?

Good Company

Curious and cheerful
Squawking with glee
A parrot swooped by to check on me
"Oh!" squealed my grandma
"How lucky are you
Parrots are cupid's chariot too"

A crow jostled him away
Cawing warning shots to obey
"Really?" asked grandma across the room
"That's very nice to hear
Crows tell of unannounced company, dear"

He spotted a friend, and off he flew
A flutter of sparrows arrived on cue
"Excellent news!" grandma approved
"Sparrows are bringers of balance and joy
What a good day this will be. O boy!"

She topped up the seeds and sugar in stripes
Calling encouragingly to all to take a bite
And in the corner, quietly she laid
Peanuts, guavas, and figs in the shade

In an instant, we were joined by soft hands
Grins, tails and a monkey band
"Now, we'll sit down to finish our tea
With good company for us, don't you agree?"

Sleuthing

Maya's elective
Was to be a detective
And a solver of mysteries

Even though she was five
She had focus and drive
The girl will make history

Right after school
She was no fool
At home she'd peer at the trash

And carefully count
The wrapper amount
Then to her Dad she would dash

Dad, she would say
Are there chocolates today?
My lunch box didn't have any

When he'd shrug or hum no
Then she'd begin apropos
With the wrapper evidence of many

"Where is my share?
And who did dare
To eat thirty-two sweets?

I check before school
As a rule
I inventory all the treats"

Her parents were distressed
Of this seeming theft
Hiding their chocolatey grins

But what they didn't know
Is Maya long ago
Put slime where the chocs had been

Number One Auntie

My Auntie taught me to rock
Over sunny afternoons
We took centre stage and danced
To the boom chicka chicka boom boom

She taught me the Twist in a minute
And how to freestyle to any tune
There isn't a song we didn't dance to
In my Auntie's bedroom

My love of elephants is enormous
Much like their rotund tums
With Auntie, a shopping I'd go
Now I have twenty-one

And when a pup was off the table
No matter the cases pleaded
Auntie nominated her Snowy
A fluffy friend – just what I needed

Auntie is a connoisseur
Treasures she can quickly spot
Pearls, rubies or glass beads
In Auntie's hands they look hot

Warm welcomes, scented with laughter
Auntie is kind
Guests are overwhelmed
With sweet notes and love sublime:

*"Live life well and joyfully
Dance every chance you get"*
Auntie has good advice
"Live life without regret"

An instant favourite with beaus
Over sweet pastries and coffee
Auntie rules hearts
With good gossip – a guarantee!

Long walks in the club
Over chicken sandwiches and chatter
Auntie is my favourite aunt
The one who really matters

Magic Carpet

Enid Blyton had a magic chair
Aladdin a magic lamp
Magic beans changed Jack's life
A magic mirror spoke to the King's wife

A magic cow and a magic horn
Were the cornucopia of India and Greece
Harry had an invisibility cape
From sparkling magic you can't escape

Alice had magic biscuits and potions
That changed her size
Cinderella a fairy godmother
Got her into balls with no bother

I have all this and a talking bear
Like Christopher's Pooh
And a hobbit's ring or two
To make the impossible true

I have tried every enchanted chair
And every charmed carpet too
Planted all our magical beans
Whispered at mirrors and screens

I have eaten all the spell binding biscuits
And spoken to our neighbourhood cow
There is magic in everything I see
Mom, do you believe me?

I'm on my magic carpet
There are no seat belts
Hold on tight and low
We're about to go go go

This isn't a flight of fancy
Join me quick, it's adventure time
Why do you sprout so many doubts?
Tell me, are you in or out?

Your fussing took too long
The magic carpet is gone

Vexations

What Will You Be?

When you grow up
What will you be?
I'd like to be just me

Will you be a doctor, lawyer
Or banking czar?
I'd like to be free like Renoir

Will you audit books
Or climb corporate ladders?
I want to do things that make me gladder

Will you be a techie, scientist or scribe?
A teacher or do comedy live?
Can't I do all five?

> *I want to help people*
> *I want to be kind*
> *I want to expand and grow my mind*
>
> *I want to see the world*
> *And dance and sway*
> *I want to learn something new every day*
>
> *I want to laugh*
> *I want to innovate*
> *I want to hug humanity and celebrate*
>
> *Is there a job*
> *That will do all this?*
> *I'll create one and live in bliss*

Circles

I think I'm running in circles
I've been here before
Different faces
But the same score

Same old competition
About kids, tech and rights
Same old excuses
A very familiar fight

I'm sure I've heard this all
Just in different words
Gosh I'm sounding like
A prophetic old bird

Did I learn my lesson
Am I making the same mistakes?
Do I need a shake up
Or just a long break?

Would I like to travel instead
Up a straight line?
Would that mean
Leaving my friends behind?

Some circles take a lifetime
Some a few years
The best circles are the ones
That ascend the stratosphere

Kite

I ponder my friend across the way
And he looks right back at me
He has much to share
Of the news of the world
And all that he did see

He saw yogis on high
Tottering on one leg
And a thousand meals being cooked
A war, a love story and dancing dwarfs
All neighbours, like in a book

He must speak up
as the parrots drown him out
And cooing pigeons are prancing nearby
The seagulls join in, O what a din!
He trills...
        ... and silence falls, for the king of the sky

Skyline

What a perfect sunset
A blushing sky and warm breeze
Gently silhouetting coconut trees

The same warm laughter
The same soft beach
Swooping birds with the same screech

The waves lap upon the shore
Jet lagged eyes open again
I'm so happy to be home, and then

Unsure I'm in Bombay
The skyline winks at me
Is it Monrovia or Panama City?

Bali or Barcelona?
Or some place new?
O gosh, I haven't a clue

I'm home when I'm with you
But doppelganger skylines
Are comforting too

Outgrown

You're kind
You're wonderful
You're true
But we must say adieu

Our paths have diverged
Our thinking too
Reminiscing
Is all we do

Outgrown
Outmatched
Exceeded
Ready to detach

A cherished friendship
This will always be
I've added a few layers
And I'm loving the new me

All this change
Has left you behind
You think it a challenge
That I grow my mind

But flex I must
Wings must be spread
Mistakes lovingly made
On a new path to tread

Not all relationships
Are forever
Not all love
Is for the ages

This was always dating
With an expiration date
Let's cut the cord
It's not up for debate

You were plan B
I didn't realise
Until we said
Our goodbyes

Farewell my friend
Thanks for exiting on cue
Life is happier
Without you

Duelling in Verse

It is my, and my privilege alone
To share my joy with you
If it makes you smile
That's a job well done
And increases my joy times two

If my joy brings you pain, that would be a shame
But my joy it would not be halved
It's with love I create
So please do appreciate:
My offer of magic above

Selfish, uncaring, unkind
Oh, what you must think of me!
I am so happy you are reading this rhyme
And thinking of a duel over tea

And as you begin your verse
All the judgement, it melts away
You'll see as I do, you are happy
And nothing can get in the way

Acknowledgements

Thank you, in any language, said infinite times, sometimes simply isn't enough. Especially for these wonderful people who have made my world, and this book possible:

My parents and my haven, Usha and Ashok Bhandarkar, for being my first glowing reviewers, cheerleaders and pure magic. Thank you for making the impossible attainable, and life so beautiful.

My heart and partner Jeevan, whose curious mind, kindness, surprising perspectives and unflinching encouragement makes me grateful every day.

To our little one Aadi, who inspired a rereading of all my favourite poets and the discovery of new joyful ones too. Thank you for being my north star.

To Lauren Anderson, Akhila Khanna, Lea Hakim, Fatima Sham-Mahimwala, Natasha Shah, and Elsa Douineau-Le Blanc for giggling out loud and the early undeserved applause – turning me from a doodling rhymester to a published poet. Your conviction gave me courage. Thank you.

To the infinite love and joyful support of my: grandparents Shanta and SS Bhandarkar, Maya and Lachu Shivdasani; family Sumithra, PV and Swathi Reddy; and number one Aunt, Asha Masi. Thank you for sharing your light with me.

Thank you to all the family and friends for the meandering chats, serendipitous adventures, and unbridled laughter. This book is in ardent appreciation of all the goodness you bring into the world. Special thanks to Nishad Avari, Madeline Craig, Neha Katyal, Siddhi Ghatlia, and Mita Sen.

Thank you to the brilliant team at Atmosphere Press for turning my book into a reality: Colleen Alles, Ronaldo Alves, and Alex Kale your warmth, time and exuberance is valued.

About the Author

Malika Bhandarkar

MALIKA has spent about two decades with the United Nations in New York, reimagining the world for people, planet, and prosperity. Though an economist by training from Yale, at heart she is an optimist and poet. An ardent explorer, she soaks in all that the worlds of science, art, literature, and travel have to offer.

Born and brought up in Bombay, India, Malika remains inspired by the rhymes, wit and philosophy of Dr. Seuss, Ogden Nash, Roald Dahl, Shel Silverstein, Judith Viorst, Erma Bombeck, James Finn Garner, Jeff Moss, Chris Harris, Erin Hanson, Vikram Seth, Khalil Gibran, Rumi, Hafiz and more.

It's Tough Being A Grown Up! is Malika's debut book of humourous observational poetry.

Some early global recognition of poems in this book include special mentions in the 2022 Tulip Tree Humor Contest for "Pounce-ciations" and 2023 Minds Shine Bright competition for "The Importance of Name Tags." Malika is also a member of the Society of Children's Book Writers and Illustrators (SCBWI).

www.ingramcontent.com/pod-product-compliance
Lightning Source LLC
Chambersburg PA
CBHW031959140726
47988CB00019B/2792